Table of Contents

Getting Started 2
Flowers and Their Parts 4
Wind, Bees, and Birds 8
Flowers to Fruit 12
Index 16

by Eric Michaels

Getting Started

Flowers are beautiful! Many of them are bright and colorful. Some of them even smell pretty. We grow flowers in our gardens. We send them to people we love. But a flower is more than just a beautiful creation. A flower has an important job in the life of a plant.

What are the different parts of a flower called? How do flowers produce seeds? And how do flowers help bring us the fruit we enjoy eating? Let's find out!

Flowers and Their Parts

Long ago, all flowers were wildflowers. They grew everywhere—in fields, in jungles, and even in some of the coldest places on Earth. Over time, people learned how to grow flowers. Today, people all over the world have flower gardens.

A flower is a **blossom**, and most flowers have **petals**. But there's more to flowers than just the petals. A flower has many parts.

You can use this diagram to locate the different parts of a flower.

The outer part of the flower is called the *calyx* (KAY-liks). It is made of leafy parts called *sepals*. The sepals are helpful. They protect the inside of the flower as it grows.

Inside the flower are two main parts: the *stamens* and the *pistil*. These parts work together. The stamens make **pollen**. When pollen lands on the pistil, seeds can grow.

Wind, Bees, and Birds

When pollen lands on a flower's pistil, this is called **pollination** (paw-luh-NAY-shuhn).

How does pollination happen in most kinds of flowers? The pollen from one flower gets to another flower of the same kind. For example, the pollen from one tulip is carried to another tulip.

How is the pollen carried? Sometimes wind carries the pollen from flower to flower. Or, pollen may be carried by honeybees!

Honeybees use pollen for food. As bees collect the pollen, some of it sticks to their bodies. That pollen is carried to other flowers as the bees fly from plant to plant.

Birds help to pollinate flowers, too. Hummingbirds help to pollinate a lot of flowers!

Hummingbirds have long beaks. They poke their beaks into flowers to drink something called *nectar*. Nectar is a liquid that is inside a flower. As the hummingbird drinks the nectar, pollen sticks to its beak. Then that pollen is carried by the hummingbird to another plant.

Flowers to Fruit

The **fruit** is the part of a plant that contains seeds. There are many different kinds of fruit. But when we talk about fruit, we usually mean the healthful food that we like to eat.

How does fruit form? Each flower has seeds in it. The part of the flower that covers the seeds swells and grows. That covering protects the seeds. It also makes a tasty food for us to enjoy!

Most fruit grows on trees, bushes, or vines. And most fruit flowers are quite small. Have you ever seen a whole **orchard** of fruit trees in bloom? All of those small flowers blooming together can be beautiful!

Flowers are important to all of us. Without them, plants could not form seeds to make new plants. We wouldn't have delicious fruit to eat. And the world would be a lot less colorful!

Index

birds, 8, 11

blossom, 4

calyx, 5, 6

fruit, 2, 12, 14, 15

gardens, 2, 4

honeybees, 8, 9

hummingbird(s), 11

nectar, 11

orchard, 14

petal(s), 4, 5

pistil, 5, 7, 8

plant(s), 2, 9, 11, 12, 15

pollen, 7–9, 11

pollination, 8

seed(s), 2, 7, 12, 13, 15

sepal(s), 5, 6

stamen(s), 5, 7

stem, 5, 6

wildflowers, 4

wind, 8